SHOW ME HOW
I Can Make Magic

Easy conjuring tricks for kids, shown step by step

HUGH NIGHTINGALE

ARMADILLO

This edition is published by Armadillo, an imprint of Anness Publishing Ltd

www.armadillobooks.co.uk; www.annesspublishing.com; twitter: @Anness_Books

If you like the images in this book and would like to investigate using them for publishing, promotions or advertising, please visit our website www.practicalpictures.com for more information.

Publisher: Joanna Lorenz
Project Editors: Judith Simons and Richard McGinlay
Additional Tricks: Nick Huckleberry Beak
Photographers: John Freeman, with Tim Ridley
Designer: Michael R. Carter
Production Controller: Stephanie Moe

ACKNOWLEDGEMENTS
We would like to thank the following children, their parents, and Brian Sharman at St. John the Baptist C. E. Primary School: Abayomi, Alexander, Aribibia, Carl, Charli, Emma, Gerald, Jonathan, Justine, Lucy, Michael, Michelle, Nhat Han, Nicola, Sarah, Scott, Stella-Rae, Tope, Trevor and Wura.

PUBLISHER'S NOTE
The amount of help needed from adults will depend on the abilities and ages of the children following the projects. However, we advise that adult supervision is vital when the project calls for the use of sharp knives or other utensils. Always keep potentially harmful tools well out of the reach of young children.
Although the advice and information in this book are believed to be accurate and true at the time of going to press, neither the authors nor the publisher can accept any legal responsibility or liability for any errors or omissions that may have been made nor for any inaccuracies nor for any loss, harm or injury that comes about from following instructions or advice in this book.

Manufacturer: Anness Publishing Ltd, 108 Great Russell Street, London WC1B 3NA, England
For Product Tracking go to: www.annesspublishing.com/tracking
Batch: 1385-23378-1127

Contents

Introduction

So, you want to be a magician? That's good! Because magic is fun. Actually, it is *great* fun. Making the tricks is fun, doing the tricks is fun and, most of all, entertaining people with magic is fun.

Some people, and books, say magic is very hard to do because it needs hour after hour, year after year, of never-ending practice. Well, in this book you will find lots of tricks that you will be able to do easily with only a little practice. And once you've learned how to do all the projects shown here, you might go on to learn the more complicated secrets of magic.

Making Things For Your Magic

The Wand

In order to make magic, you need a few essential props. The most important of these is your wand. You can make one yourself. All you need is a 30cm/12in length of round wood, called dowel, some masking tape and black and white poster paints. Wrap masking tape around each end of the dowel and paint the wood in-between black. When the paint is dry, remove the tape and paint the ends white. Hey presto! The stick has magically become a wand, ready for you to do some brilliant tricks with.

The Magic Box

An essential prop is a beautifully decorated magic box. This box means you will be able to produce many things you need for your show, out of a box that seems to be empty!

1 First tape over the sharp edges of an empty 850g/28oz baked bean can. Glue a rectangle of thin red cardboard together at the edges, to make a tube wider and taller than the can. For the outer box, join four identical pieces of stiff cardboard with masking tape. Ask a grown-up to help you cut out some holes in one piece for the front of the box.

2 Here Lucy has decorated the box to look like an old-fashioned radio. Now paint half of the bean can and the inside of the box with black poster paint. When the paint is dry, fill the can with magical things.

3 Put the bean can, filled with silk handkerchiefs, cards, a small pink rabbit and a plastic fried egg, inside the box. Can you see it? No? That is because you place it in the box with its black side facing the holes in the front, so when you lift out the red tube the box appears empty. After putting the red tube back over the bean can, you can lift up the radio box, because it has no bottom, to show that it is empty as well.

4 This "illusion" means that Lucy can produce the hankies, cards and rabbit from an "empty" box. She is able to turn the can around when it is inside the tube and lift it out, with the egg, to add a funny finish to her trick. Now, once she has put the can and egg away, she can again show her audience that the tube and box are both empty. This time, because there is nothing left to hide, she can hold the tube and box up together.

The Hat

Every self-respecting magician has a top hat, and it is needed for many of the tricks in this book.

1 Ask a friend to measure around your head. Add 2cm/1in to the figure and cut a piece of stiff black paper to this length, and about 15cm/6in wide. Roll the paper into a tube and glue the edges together.

2 For the top of the hat, place the tube upright on a sheet of black paper and draw round it with a white crayon. Draw a second circle about 1cm/½in wider around the first circle and cut out the outer line. Cut small "V"s around the whole shape between the outer and inner circles. Glue the tabs downwards inside the top of the tube. To make the brim, draw round the shape of your hat on to more black paper. Draw a second circle 1cm/½in smaller than your tube and a third circle 5cm/2in larger. Cut out along these last two lines. Cut tabs again and glue them into the bottom of your hat.

3 A secret flap fixed inside your magician's top hat is perfect for hiding things. Cut out a round piece of stiff black paper to fit snugly down into the hat. Tape a flap on to the middle of it with masking tape. Paint the tape black and cut the flap into a semicircle so that it can be held against either side of the hat, with your fingers. If you briefly tip the opening of the hat towards the audience, anything hidden behind the flap will not be seen. They will just see blackness inside the hat and assume the hat is empty.

4 Add some ribbon to the hat to finish it off. Measure round the tube of your hat, and add 1cm/½in to this. Glue the ribbon round the hat just above the brim with a 1cm/½in overlap. Wearing a bow tie will make you really look like a magician.

Performing

Performing magic is all about acting the part of the magician convincingly. When you are doing a trick you must try to believe that magic is really happening. If you believe it, so will your audience.

What to Say

What you say to your audience during your show is called your "patter". The most important thing is to be natural. Talk in your own way. Make up a story to go with the trick and add a few jokes if you would like to get a laugh.

Repeating Tricks

When you have done a good trick, people will ask to see it again. Don't be tempted to repeat it! Your audience might discover the secret of the trick the second time round.

Misdirection

This is the art of making your audience look where *you* want them to look. The audience will look where your eyes are looking or at your moving hands. If you are hiding a coin in your hand, don't look at that hand. Also, never say that a box or hat is "empty" or the audience will be suspicious. Quickly show them the inside and they will assume that it is empty.

Secrets

Always keep your magic secrets to yourself. Store your magic things out of sight, in a case or a closed box.

Appearance

Look well presented and especially have clean hands and fingernails. Smile. Look happy. If you feel a little shy in front of an audience, try your tricks out in private first, and even in front of a mirror.

Mistakes

Sometimes things will go wrong – even the most famous magicians sometimes make mistakes! Don't panic. If you can, correct things and carry on. If you can't, just smile and get the audience involved in another trick. Remember that your audience is there because they want to be entertained and they want you to do well. Trying out your tricks in front of a mirror will help prevent the mistakes from happening.

Magic Secrets

Part of the skill of being a magician is keeping things to yourself. In order to show how to do things, we have taken photographs, but whenever you see the top hat symbol, this is a view that the audience should not see.

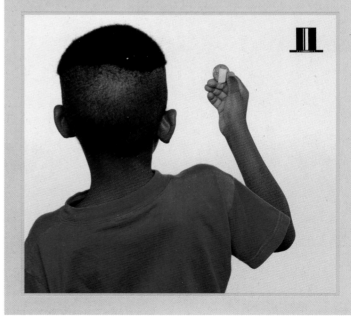

How Many Tricks?

Don't make your show too long. That way you will leave your audience wanting more and they will ask you for another show on another day. Plan a short show that has a beginning, a middle and an end. And don't forget – smile!

Magic Words

In magic there are many special words. Here are some useful ones for you to learn.

EFFECT What the audience sees.

GAG A joke or a funny story.

GIMMICK OR FAKE A secret part of the prop that the audience does not see.

ILLUSION When something *seems* to happen but doesn't.

LOAD The things held in a secret compartment.

PALMING Keeping something hidden in your hand.

PATTER Your talk that goes with the trick.

PRODUCTION Making something appear from nowhere.

PROPS The things you use for your tricks.

ROUTINE A series of tricks or moves.

SHUFFLE To mix up cards in your hands.

SILKS Silk handkerchiefs.

SLEEVING Hiding something up your sleeve to make it vanish or ready to appear in your hand later.

SLEIGHT OF HAND A clever movement of your hand to make magic.

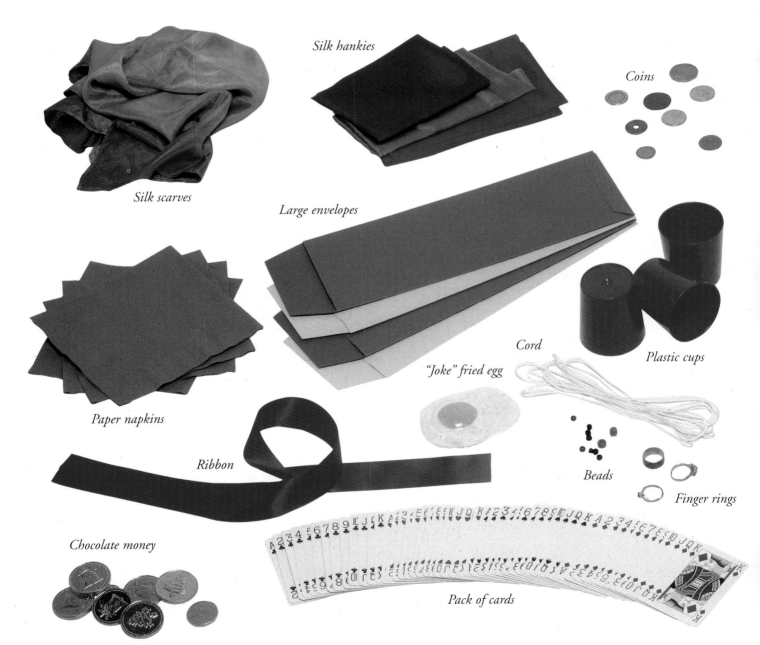

Silk scarves

Silk hankies

Coins

Large envelopes

Paper napkins

"Joke" fried egg

Cord

Plastic cups

Ribbon

Beads

Finger rings

Chocolate money

Pack of cards

STEAL To move something from its place secretly.
SWITCH To change one thing for another secretly.
TALK The sound that hidden objects might make – for example, rattle, click, etc.
TRANSPOSITION When something magically disappears from one place to reappear in another.
VANISH To make an object seem to disappear.

Materials

The materials that you will need are always listed. Gather them all together before you start. Work on a suitable surface. Wear an apron if you are painting or gluing, and clear everything away afterwards. Allow time for paint and glue to dry before moving on to the next stage. Keep a collection of empty cartons, tubes and boxes, etc. Once they have been painted and decorated they are great for magic. Take great care when using scissors or other sharp instruments, and always ask a grown-up to help if you need to use a craft knife.

Black is very useful in magic because a black object in black surroundings becomes almost invisible. So, if the instructions for a trick say to use black, then *do* use black. Finally, take your time and study the photographs and the text carefully. If a photograph shows someone doing a trick with their right hand and you prefer to use your left, don't worry. Just swap things over and do it your own way.

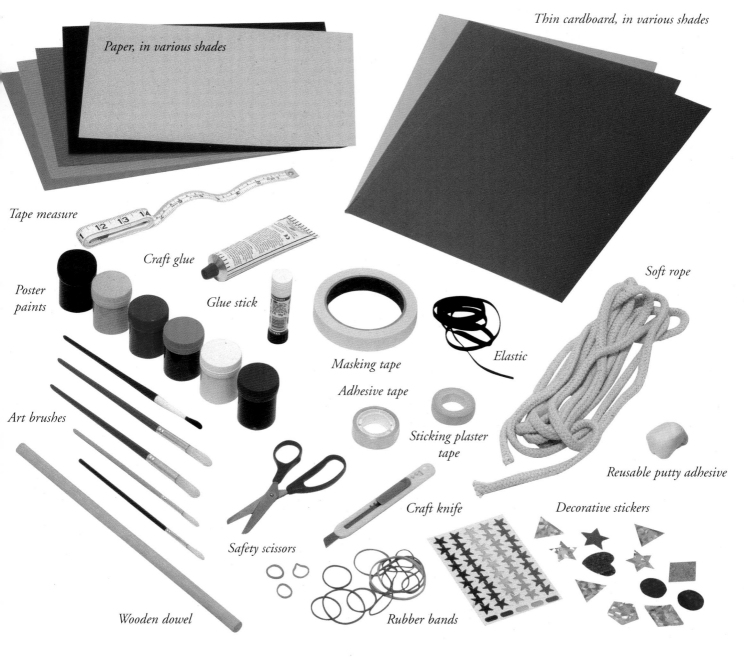

Paper, in various shades

Thin cardboard, in various shades

Tape measure

Craft glue

Glue stick

Poster paints

Masking tape

Adhesive tape

Elastic

Soft rope

Art brushes

Sticking plaster tape

Reusable putty adhesive

Safety scissors

Craft knife

Decorative stickers

Wooden dowel

Rubber bands

Hanky Pranky

Wouldn't it be fun to borrow a small object from a friend, like a coin, place it on your handkerchief, give it a little rub and – it disappears! It would be even better, for your friend, if you could make it come back again. This trick needs very little preparation, so it is just the job for when a friend says, "Go on, then, show us a trick." You only need a rubber band and a large hanky, or you might be able to borrow the hanky (if it's clean!). You can make all sorts of small objects vanish with this method, but Charli likes to do the trick with a ring.

Tip
Keep a few rubber bands in your pocket, so that you are always prepared.

YOU WILL NEED THESE PROPS

Small rubber bands

Medium to large silk hanky (patterned is best)

Small objects

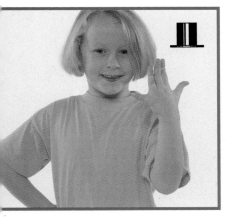

1 Secretly put the rubber band round the tips of three fingers of your left hand. Take out the silk hanky, but don't let anyone see the rubber band.

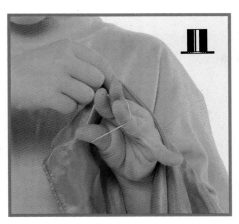

2 Quickly spread the hanky over your left hand to hide the band. Secretly slip your thumb into the band to open it out. Ask to borrow a ring.

3 Show everyone the ring, then place it on the silk over where the rubber band is. Rub the ring with your free hand to push it through the band.

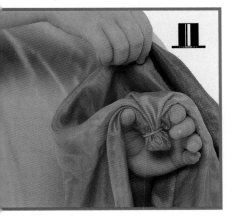

4 Slip the band off your fingers to trap the ring in a fold in the silk. This is the "magic" bit, so don't let anyone see you do this!

5 Now whip the silk away and stare at your empty left hand. Where has the ring gone?

6 When you want to make the ring reappear, spread the silk over your left hand, reach into the folds with your right hand, and pull out the ring.

13

Tricky Tubes

This is a classic trick used by magicians everywhere. It involves moving a handkerchief from one "magic" tube to another to give the impression that both tubes are empty.
In the finale of this illusion, you stun the audience by producing a handkerchief from the empty tubes.

YOU WILL NEED THESE PROPS

2 pieces of 30cm x 30cm/ 12in x 12in thin cardboard in different shades

Rubber band

Small handkerchief

9 paperclips

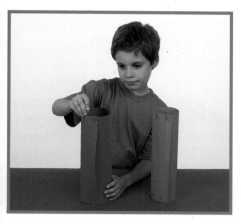

1 Steps 1, 2 and 3 show what you have to do to prepare for this trick. Roll the pieces of cardboard to make tubes. One tube must be slightly narrower so that it will fit inside the larger tube. Secure the tubes with eight paperclips.

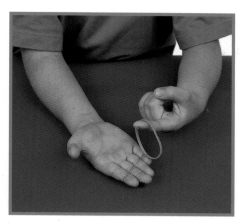

2 The device that makes this trick work is a paperclip. Unfold the paperclip to make hooks at either end, as shown. Attach a rubber band to one hook. Roll up the handkerchief and thread it into the rubber band.

3 Hook the other end of the paperclip on to the top of the narrow tube. The rubber band and the handkerchief will be on the inside of the tube. Make sure that the handkerchief is totally hidden from view.

4 Now it is time to get this show on the road! Hold up the large tube so that the audience can see that it is completely empty. This should not be difficult as it really is empty!

5 Pick up the narrow tube and slide it slowly down through the large tube. As you do this, the paperclip holding the handkerchief will hook itself on to the large tube.

6 Pull the narrow tube out from the bottom of the large tube. Then, with a flourish, hold up the narrow tube to show your audience that it is empty.

7 Place the narrow tube on the table. Slide the large tube over the narrow tube. The handkerchief will fall inside the narrow tube. Then say to your audience, "From two empty tubes, I will magically produce a handkerchief." Pull the handkerchief from inside the narrow tube. All you have to do now is wait for the applause and take a bow!

Money from Nowhere!

Tip

For your special coin, to save it from melting, carefully take the chocolate out of the foil and make it vanish, in your mouth! Replace it with a circle of cardboard and you can use the coin over and over again.

How about this for a trick? You are holding your empty top hat in one hand, then, with the other hand, you reach up and pluck a gold coin out of the air and drop it into your hat. Then you find another in the air, then another and another. Aribibia is finding coins all over the place, even behind people's ears! Finally he tips his hat on to the table and out pours a shower of golden coins. There are enough coins to hand out to friends after the show. When you do this trick, you will use a specially prepared coin, so make sure you do not give it away but keep it safely for next time.

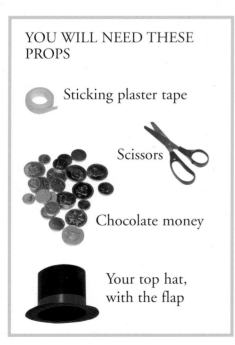

YOU WILL NEED THESE PROPS

Sticking plaster tape

Scissors

Chocolate money

Your top hat, with the flap

1 Before you start the trick, fix about 4cm/1½in of sticking plaster to one side of your special coin, leaving about 2cm/½in hanging free.

2 Load one side of your hat flap with chocolate money. With the flap over the money, you can show your audience that the hat is "empty".

3 Hold the coin between your finger and thumb with the plaster stuck to your second and third fingers. Keep the back of your hand to the audience.

4 Hold your hand over the hat, and let the coin go. It will fall behind your fingers, but the audience will believe it has fallen into the hat.

5 Flick the coin up again, and catch it with your thumb. You've caught a coin from the air! Drop it into the hat. Repeat this action several times.

6 Shake the hat to rattle the coins that are already in it. The audience will be convinced that you have caught a hatful of coins from thin air.

7 Finally pour the coins on to the table to show just how many you have collected from thin air.

Magic Wands

It always looks good, in your show, to wave your wand whenever you wish the "magic" to happen. Nhat Han has also discovered some tricks that use the wand itself. She can make the wand "magnetic" – it will cling to her hand with, apparently, nothing holding it in place. She can, or so it appears, push the wand right into her leg and it doesn't hurt her. She can also make her wand stiff one minute and bendy the next. How does she do that?

YOU WILL NEED THESE PROPS

Your wand, or a pencil

White paper

Scissors

Glue stick

Magnetic Wand

1 If you are holding a wand and you open your hand, it falls to the floor. Oh, dear!

2 But if you are a magician, like Nhat Han, it will stay in your hand all by itself.

3 Look on the other side of her hand. Can you see her secret? Try it yourself.

Painless Wand

1 Nhat Han rolls up a piece of white paper and glues it to make a tube the same size as the tip of her wand.

2 Nhat Han has pushed the wand right into her leg! But it did not seem to hurt! How did she do that?

3 She hid the lower wand tip in her hand and pushed the paper tube down the wand with her other hand.

Wobbly Wand

1 Nhat Han is trying to bend her wand. It is definitely stiff.

2 Next, she holds it loosely between finger and thumb, about one third of the way down. When she moves it from side to side, it looks wobbly.

Stringy Strange

YOU WILL NEED THESE PROPS

Fine cord

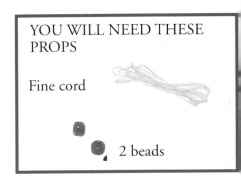

2 beads

Nicola has a really weird piece of string. She can make it pass through solid metal, glass or china. She can even make it pass through her friend Scott's arm! To make a piece of magic string like Nicola's, simply thread two small beads on to about 60cm/24in of strong fine cord and tie a large knot at each end. Ask your friends to examine it closely, to satisfy themselves that it is a solid piece of string.

Tip

Use beads that are small enough to hide behind your fingertips.

We have let you see the beads in the photographs, but don't let your audience see them, when you perform.

You could try out the trick on the wooden arm of a chair before you try it on a friend or in front of other people.

1 Hold the two beads, one at each end of the cord, in one hand.

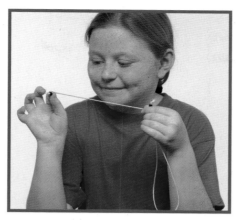

2 Take one bead in the other hand and pull the cord out as shown.

3 Fully extend the cord to show the audience that it is long and strong, and that there is a bead at each end.

4 Hold the two beads in one hand, as in Step 1. Then pull only the knot with the other hand, leaving the two beads together in your left hand.

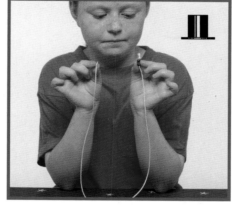

5 Hold the two ends close together, so the audience think it is the same as in Step 1. In fact both beads are at one end of the cord, but one is hidden.

6 Get a friend to link his arms. Hold both ends of the cord in one hand. Put your free hand through his arms and take hold of the "knot-only" end.

7 Pull on the cord and move your hands together and then apart several times. Then take hold of a bead in each hand (without anyone seeing).

8 Quickly pull your hands apart, let go of the knot end and pull the bead back down to the other end of the cord, all in one go.

9 The cord will fly around your friend's arm so fast that it won't be seen. The audience will think that the cord passed right through the arm!

The Coin Fold

Tricks with money always get the audience's attention, especially if you make the money disappear and it belongs to someone in the audience! Alexander finds that the coin fold shown here is a very useful method for helping to make a coin vanish easily. But he had to rehearse long and hard to perfect his technique, especially making the coin reappear from Michelle's ear.

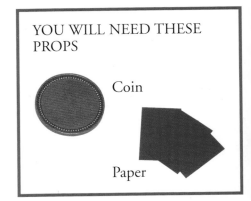

YOU WILL NEED THESE PROPS

Coin

Paper

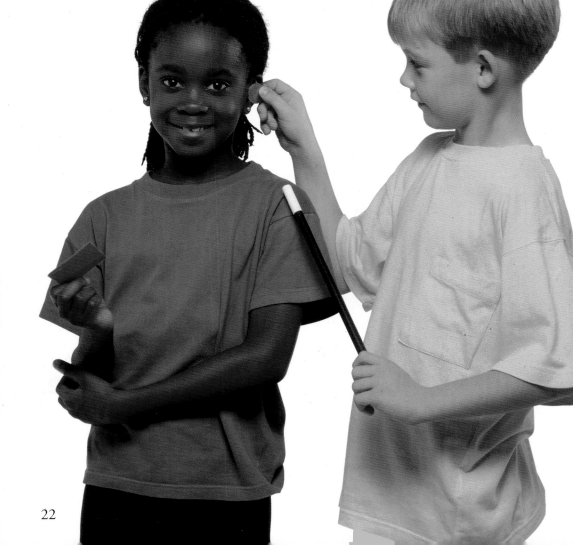

Tip

Because the audience sees you wrap the coin in the paper, their eyes stay on the paper packet. This "misdirection" allows you to drop the coin into your hand.

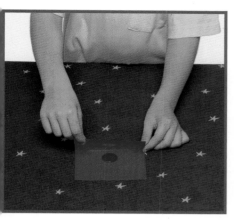

1 Place the coin in the middle of the paper and fold about one-third of the paper over it.

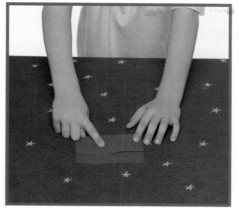

2 Press this down. It helps if you leave a coin-shaped impression in the paper.

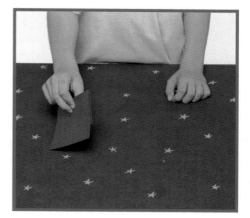

3 Turn the paper and coin over, carefully, holding the coin in the fold of the paper, as Alexander is doing here.

4 Fold over about one-third from one side.

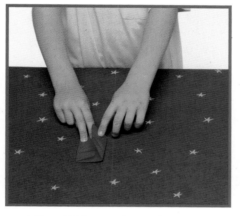

5 Then fold over about the same from the other side, so that the folds overlap.

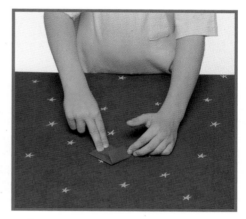

6 Now fold the flap at the top over the other folds. Put the package in your left hand and hold a corner of the flap with your left thumb.

7 Gently lift the package, so that the coin slides out of the secret gap and stays hidden in your hand. Hold it with your second and third fingers.

8 Now you can tear up the package in front of the audience. Or you can hand it to a friend to hold, and pretend to find the coin in her ear.

Cutting Coins

Here is a routine that uses the coin fold principle demonstrated in the previous trick, some misdirection and a technique called "sleeving" the coin. The trick is a bit complicated to do, and might need a lot of practice. But if you can do this trick successfully, everyone will be convinced that you really *are* a magician. You will need to wear a jacket, blazer or similar clothing, with an inside breast pocket. Look at the pictures carefully. Notice in particular how Lucy uses her eyes to draw the audience's attention to exactly where she wants them to look, while she is doing the secret move somewhere else.

Tip

Put the scissors in your breast pocket before you start the routine. Place them point down. If you borrow the coin, you could get the lender to sign it with a felt-tipped pen, or remember the date on the coin. This will prove that you are using only one coin.

All the time you are performing the trick, keep your eyes on the packet to misdirect your audience.

YOU WILL NEED THESE PROPS

Coin

Pad of paper

Blunt-ended scissors

Jacket with inside breast pocket

1 Borrow a coin and do the coin fold as described in Steps 1 to 7 in the previous trick. Keep the coin hidden in your right hand.

2 Reach into your breast pocket for the scissors, but first drop the coin into your sleeve. Keep your arm bent up, so the coin stays near the elbow.

3 Bring out the scissors and cut the packet into little pieces. The coin has vanished! (You know it is in your sleeve by your elbow.)

4 Make up another little packet, keeping your arm with the coin bent. The audience can see that your hands, and the paper, are empty.

5 Rattle the packet and listen to it. Look as if you can hear a coin in there. This misdirects the audience while you drop your left hand naturally to your side. Catch the coin with your fingers as it slides out of your sleeve.

6 Keeping the coin hidden, bring both hands together and quickly tear open the paper packet. The coin that was hidden in your fingers seems to come out of the empty packet.

There's more monetary mayhem in Coin Through Hand, later on in the book!

The Amazing Jumping Rubber Band

Tip
Rehearse getting all four fingertips into the rubber band with the minimum of movement. It should look, to the audience, as if you are just making the band comfortable on your fingers.

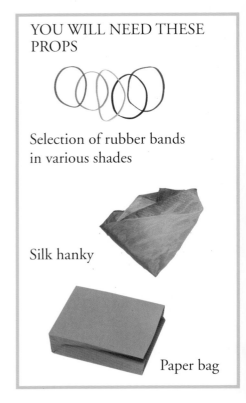

YOU WILL NEED THESE PROPS

Selection of rubber bands in various shades

Silk hanky

Paper bag

These rubber band tricks show off your incredible skills at sleight of hand but they are very easy to do, as Abayomi has found out. First of all, a rubber band "jumps" from your first and second fingers, to your third and fourth, in less time than the blink of an eye. Next, two bands swap places on your fingers in the time it takes to wave a silk hanky over your hand. Finally, the bands swap places yet again, even though you have tied all your fingers together with a third band. The really good news is that to do all these tricks you only have to learn one secret move. The silk hanky, the third band and the paper bag are all for "dressing up" the trick and actually have nothing to do with making it work.

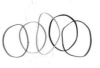

1 You apparently put a rubber band around two fingers and then close your hand.

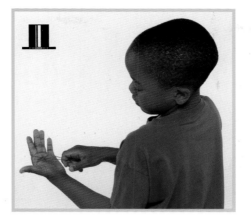

2 Actually, as you close your fingers, you pull open the rubber band.

3 Slip all four fingertips into the rubber band. Do this quickly and secretly – don't let the audience see.

4 From your side, your hand looks like this. Try it, then open and close your hand. The band jumps, automatically, to the other two fingers.

5 To make it jump back again, put all four fingertips into the band again as you close your hand. Open and close your hand.

6 If you use two different looking rubber bands and put all four fingertips into both as you close your hand, the bands swap places.

7 The rubber bands have now swapped places. Wave the silk handkerchief in front just to make the trick look more "showy".

8 Bind your fingertips together with a third band, to make the trick look virtually impossible to do.

9 Quickly put your hand in a paper bag, do the same move and pull your hand out. Hey presto! The bands have swapped places.

Middle House Mouse

This trick is loosely based on what's probably the oldest magic trick in the world, the "cups and balls", which is over 2000 years old. When Wura performs the trick using fluffy mice, she tells a story about a mouse who only ever wanted to live in a middle house, never at the end of a row.

Tip

You do not have to use mice. Look in the shops for four identical novelty animals that fit in your cups or you could even make your own.

The beakers or cups need to be of flexible plastic, not china or metal.

To make the bases for your animals, draw around a beaker on to the cardboard. Ask a grown-up to cut out the circle so that it is just a little *smaller* than the mouth of the beaker.

Never ever show more than one mouse at one time. The audience must believe that there is only one.

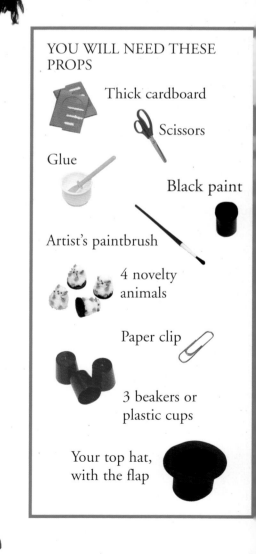

YOU WILL NEED THESE PROPS

Thick cardboard

Scissors

Glue

Black paint

Artist's paintbrush

4 novelty animals

Paper clip

3 beakers or plastic cups

Your top hat, with the flap

1 Ask a grown-up to cut out three circles to just fit inside a beaker. Paint them black. Leave to dry, then glue the circles on to the three mice.

2 Unbend the paper clip to make a hook at each end. Push one end into the fourth mouse. Hook it to your back before starting the trick.

3 Try lifting up a beaker with a mouse inside. If you squeeze the cup when you lift it, the mouse stays in the cup and seems to "disappear".

4 Now for the performance. Arrange three beakers, each with a mouse hidden inside, in a line. Show the audience only the middle mouse.

5 Squeeze the two end beakers gently as you lift them (to hold the mice inside) to show they are "empty".

6 Swap the two end beakers with the middle one. Then lift the new middle beaker to show that the mouse has magically jumped back.

7 Swap the beakers again. Take the mouse from the end cup, and put it in your top hat. Lift the middle cup. The mouse has "jumped" back again!

8 Repeat until all the mice are in the hat, then show that the hat is also "empty". The audience will see where the mouse is when you turn round!

The Dirty Napkin Trick

Magic can have the most powerful effect when people are not expecting it. Here's a trick you could do during a meal. Sarah has this trick well under control. When the person opposite her has sat down and spread his paper napkin on his knee, she asks him for the napkin. She gives the excuse that she has noticed some tiny stains on it. To do the trick she tears off pieces from the middle of the napkin, explaining each time that, "this one's gravy, this one's ketchup", and so on. Finally she opens the napkin out to show that it is whole – without any bits torn out of it. This trick is a real reputation maker. Try it yourself.

YOU WILL NEED THESE PROPS

Paper napkins

Some small rubber bands

A piece torn from the middle of an identical spare napkin

Tip

Don't use your own napkin for the secret torn piece, as someone might ask to see it afterwards. When you tear off the pieces, remove the rubber band with one of them (see step 6).

1 Secretly, under the table, attach the torn piece of napkin to the inside of your left thumb with the rubber band, so that it is hidden in your hand.

2 Borrow a napkin from another diner. No one will notice the torn piece as you reach across the table to take the napkin.

3 Spread the napkin over your left hand and point to the "stains" as you push the middle of the napkin into your hand.

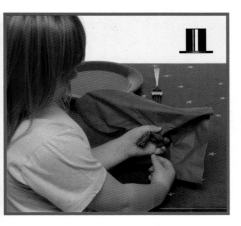

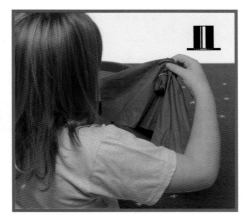

4 The real middle, and the torn middle, are side by side. Here we can see under Sarah's napkin, but don't let anyone else see what is happening.

5 Take both the middles into your right hand. Turn them upside down and put them back into your left hand. Pull up only the torn piece.

6 Tear off pieces, saying they are stained, and put them in your pocket. Remove the rubber band with one of the pieces.

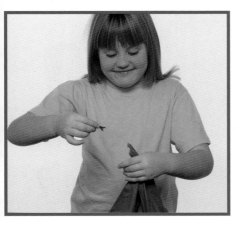

7 Really, you are tearing pieces from the extra piece in your hand. It will look as if you are tearing them from the middle of the napkin.

8 When it looks like you have thoroughly ruined the napkin, calmly open out the real napkin to the amazement of everyone at the table.

Postman's Wand

Gerald is demonstrating a really smart trick he has learned. He puts his wand into an envelope, ready to post it. Then he performs a little magic, and "alakazam", the wand disappears from the envelope and then it reappears in a different envelope on the other side of the room.

Tips

Find some large envelopes that fit your wand – in different shades if possible, or decorate them differently.

Make sure the envelopes stay in view at all times. Prop them up against the backs of two chairs if necessary.

Before you put the wand into the envelope, tap the chairs or tables with the wand. This proves that the wand is solid without your actually having to say so, which would seem suspicious.

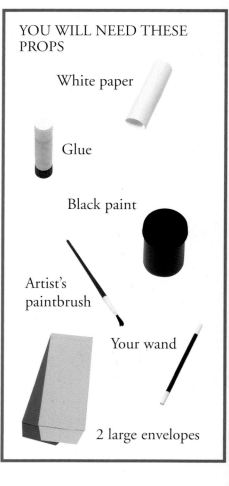

YOU WILL NEED THESE PROPS

White paper

Glue

Black paint

Artist's paintbrush

Your wand

2 large envelopes

1 Roll up some paper and glue it to make a hollow paper wand. Paint it to look like a real wand. When the paint is dry, slide it over the real wand.

2 Show your audience the two empty envelopes and place them apart on two tables or chairs.

3 Put the wand into one envelope. Shake your head and take it out, secretly letting the real wand slide out of the paper one into the envelope.

4 Put the paper wand into the other envelope, saying, "I prefer it in this one". Now the trick is done, but the audience thinks it has just started.

5 So now it is all acting. Make a magical "swapping over" sign with your arms.

6 The audience saw you put the wand in the second envelope yet you can prove it is now empty by scrunching it up into a ball.

7 With a grand gesture, open up the first envelope to reveal your real wand, which has magically moved through the air. Magician, take a bow.

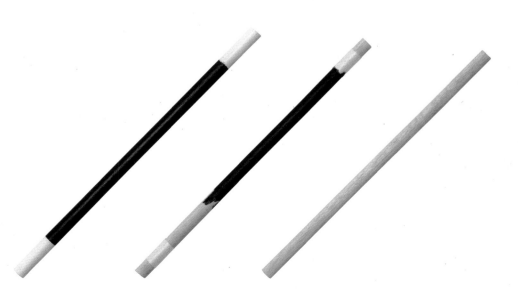

The Big Card Trick

You may have seen this trick performed many times, but now you will be able to do it for yourself. You can choose any number or suit you want for the large playing card, but you must have a card of the same number and suit at the top of your pack of cards. The two cards attached to the large card must be numerically smaller than the big card.

YOU WILL NEED THESE PROPS

Pack of playing cards and 1 large envelope

Reusable putty adhesive

Large playing card

Tip

You can make your own large playing card with thin white cardboard and a black marker pen. It does not matter which suit or number you choose to draw, so long as it is the same as the top card on your pack of cards.

34

1 To prepare for this trick, use a small piece of putty to attach a two and a four of any suit on to the back of the large ten of clubs card. Place them in the envelope. Also check that the ten of clubs is the top card on your pack of playing cards. Now let the show begin!

2 Invite someone from the audience to join you on stage and cut the pack of cards. No, not with a pair of scissors! To cut the cards, all your guest has to do is take a pile of cards off the top of the pack and lay them beside the remaining cards.

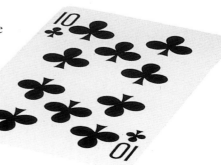

3 Place the bottom half of the pack on top of the other cards. Place it so that it is at right angles to the cut cards. This will show you where the pack was cut and where you will find the ten of clubs. Tell your guest that they will shortly see their secret card.

4 Remove the upper stack of cards from the pile and turn over the next card. Without looking at it, show it to your guest. Tell them that they must remember what their secret card is.

5 Ask your guest to shuffle the cards as much as they like. When they are shuffled, put them into the envelope. This envelope contains the large card plus the two other smaller cards.

7 Repeat the routine as in step 6, but this time pull out the four card. It is now your big moment to astound and amuse everyone. Put your hand into the envelope again and pull out the large ten of clubs card. Show it to your guest and say, "Is this big enough?" You have shown your guest that you knew that their chosen card was the ten of clubs all the time.

6 Tell your guest that you are going to find their secret card. Put your hand into the envelope and pull out the two card. Ask if this is the secret card. Of course, they will say no. Then you ask, "Is it bigger than this?"

Back-flip Card

Tip
When someone has chosen a card, ask them to show it to someone else (not you!). This helps to avoid them forgetting which card they chose, which would spoil the trick.

When people know you do magic, they will often ask to see a card trick. The trouble is, many card tricks involve complicated, finger-twisting moves. But try this – if you can put a pack of cards behind your back, turn the whole pack over and then turn just the top card over, you can do this trick. It is that easy. You have to have a reason for putting the cards behind your back, so explain that anyone can do a card trick when they can see the cards, but it takes a *real* magician to do it behind their back. Here, Michelle tries the trick out on Alexander.

YOU WILL NEED THESE PROPS

Pack of cards

1 Shuffle the cards, then hold them like a fan, face down in your hand. Ask a friend to take a card and remember it, but not to let you see it.

2 While talking about doing tricks behind your back, put the pack behind your back and turn it over. Pick off the top card.

3 Turn this card over and put it back on top of the pack. Do this quite quickly. Then bring the cards to the front again.

4 Hold the cards as a pack. All the cards are face up except the top one. Ask your friend to slide his card into the pack. Keep the pack closed.

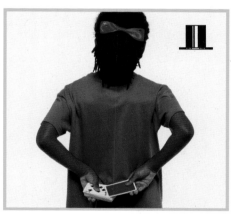

5 Put the pack behind your back again and pick off the top card.

6 Turn over the top card and put it back on the pack. Then turn the whole pack over while you say you are trying to find your friend's card.

7 Bring the pack to the front again and spread them out. Hocus-pocus! One card is face up, and yes – it is the very card that was chosen!

Coin Through Hand

An impromptu trick is one that you can do anywhere with no preparation or "props". All you need for this impromptu trick is your hands and a coin, which you can borrow. It is also very easy to do and is the first coin trick real magicians usually learn. You can really "act" this one. The audience, at first, think they have caught you out, so they are even more surprised when the coin really does end up in your fist. Michael shows us how to do it.

YOU WILL NEED THESE PROPS

Coin

Tip

Use a medium to large coin, if possible. Small, light coins sometimes stick to your fingers and do not drop when you want them to.

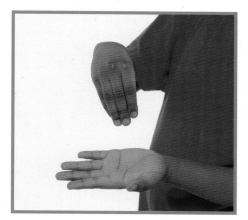

1 Hold the coin above your left fist, as shown, and announce, "I'm going to push this coin through the back of my hand."

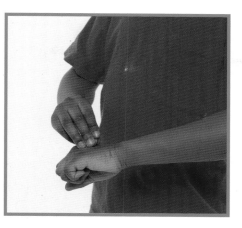

2 As you push the coin down, it slides up, out of sight behind your fingers. "There, it's gone through," you can say.

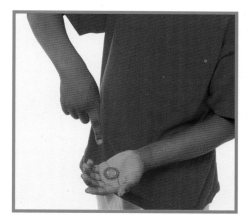

3 Open your fist and say, "Whoops! It must have got stuck halfway." The audience, though, think they know where it is.

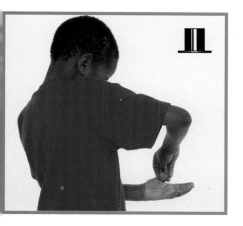

4 "I'll try again," you say as you do the sneaky bit. The sneaky bit is that, as you turn your left hand back over into a fist, your thumb almost brushes against the tips of the fingers holding the coin. Just at this point you let the coin slip out of your fingers, and you catch it in your left hand, which you make into a fist.

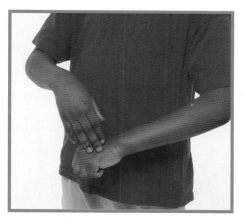

5 It all happens so quickly the audience believe it is still hidden behind your fingers, and you say, "I'll give it a harder push this time."

6 Now slowly turn your fist over and open it up. "Ah, there it is!"

Purple Hanky, Red Hanky

Tips
If you choose volunteers who are wearing clothes that match your silk handkerchiefs, it is easier for the audience to follow the trick and for you to remember where the different silks are all the time.

When you tear open the parcel at the end of the trick, take care not to tear too deeply or you will expose the wrong silk.

People in the audience love to come up and help during a show. For this trick, two assistants are needed. Nicola cleverly chose Scott, who was wearing a purple T-shirt, to hold the wrapped purple silk hanky, and Tope, who was wearing red, to hold the wrapped red silk hanky. Scott and Tope never let go of their parcels, but Nicola makes them keep changing sides. A wave of her wand and, "Hey presto", the hankies have changed places. Now, that *is* magic! How is it done? Well, the newspapers are not as ordinary as they seem.

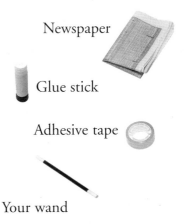

YOU WILL NEED THESE PROPS

 2 pairs of silk hankies in contrasting shades, such as red and purple

 Newspaper

Glue stick

Adhesive tape

Your wand

1 Before the show, lay out a silk handkerchief on a sheet of newspaper and spread glue round it (not on it!) with the glue stick.

2 Stick a second sheet on top. Do the same with a silk in the other shade. Make a secret mark on the papers, so you know which is which.

3 Fold up the sheets of newspapers and put them on your table, with your wand and the adhesive tape. Show the audience the remaining two silks.

4 Wrap the red silk in the paper which has the purple one hidden inside, and make a rough ball shape.

5 Use adhesive tape to hold the parcel together. Now wrap the purple silk in the paper with the red one inside, and hold it together with tape.

6 Ask for two volunteers. Give the wrapped red silk to someone wearing red, and the wrapped purple silk to someone in purple.

7 Ask your volunteers to swap places while holding on to their parcels. Wave your wand in the air to make the magic work.

8 Tear open the outer layer of the "purple" parcel. Instead of a purple silk, you pull out a red one! And from the "red" you pull out a purple silk.

41

X-ray Wand and Ringing Up

Here are two special tricks using magic wands, but with a difference. The second trick uses your wooden wand, but the first uses a hollow wand. Carl has made a hollow wand by rolling up a sheet of paper and painting it to look like a real one. The X-ray Wand routine is perfect for when you are showing a trick to just one friend, because you actually teach them how to do it. They will be amazed to see a hole right through their hand!

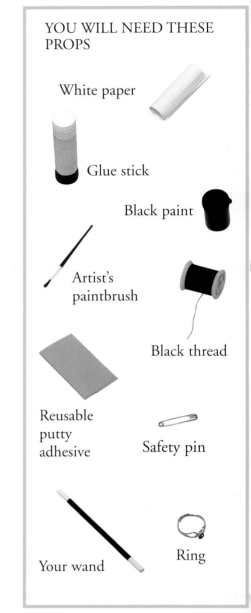

YOU WILL NEED THESE PROPS

White paper

Glue stick

Black paint

Artist's paintbrush

Black thread

Reusable putty adhesive

Safety pin

Your wand

Ring

X-ray Wand

1 Roll and glue a sheet of paper to form a tube. Then paint it to look like a wand.

2 Hold the paper wand up to your eye and look through it, keeping both eyes open.

3 Place your other hand, open flat, about halfway along it, beside the wand.

4 Now you will see a hole straight through your hand!

Ringing Up (see below) is great fun because you can use a ring that you have borrowed from someone in the audience. People always enjoy seeing their own things behaving in strange, magical ways.

Ringing Up

1 Attach a black thread to your wand with putty. Tie the thread to a safety pin and attach this to your waist. Put a ring over the wand to rest on your fist.

2 Wriggle your other fingers as you move the wand slightly away from yourself – the ring starts to rise. How?

3 As you move the wand forwards, the thread attached to your waistband and to the wand moves higher, pushing the ring up the wand.

Time-bomb Escape

How would you like to do a really dangerous and "death-defying" trick to add drama and suspense to your show? Imagine, then, being tied up in a time bomb and escaping with only seconds to spare. You could pretend to be like Houdini, who was one of the greatest magicians and escapologists of all time. Before you start, ask a grown-up to make a small hole on each side of the box, about halfway up, for the ropes to go through.

Tips
Decorate your box to make it look really dangerous!

Once you are shut in the box, get the audience to count down from 30 to 1 and then, if you have not escaped, to shout "Bang".

With practice, you will find you can free yourself from the ropes in only a few seconds, but do not jump out too early. The effect is much more dramatic if you leave it until there are only two or three seconds to spare!

YOU WILL NEED THESE PROPS

Large cardboard box that you can fit into

Paints

Artist's paintbrush

Shaped stickers

Long silk scarf

Two lengths of soft rope, each about 3–4m/10–13ft long

1 Ask one of your assistants to tie your hands with the scarf. Tie the scarf round one wrist, then the other next to it, firmly, but not *too* tightly.

2 Then ask your assistants to loop a rope over each of your arms. They must hold on firmly to the ends of the ropes, not letting go until the trick is completed. You will be trapped!

3 Climb into the box with an assistant standing guard on each side. Ask them to push the free ends of the ropes out through the small holes in the sides of the box, and then keep hold of them.

4 Squat down inside the box and tell your assistants to close the flaps. Now they can start the countdown with the audience: 30, 29, 28…

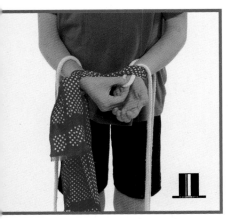

5 Even though you are tied up, you will be able to work the rope free. Pull a loop of the rope down the inside of your wrist under the silk scarf.

6 Push the loop back over your hand and let it slide up the back of your wrist. That hand is free. Now do the other one.

7 With only a few seconds of the countdown to spare, jump up like a jack-in-the-box, holding your arms in the air to show they are free.

The Wonder Tree

For the last trick in the book, here is an effect that will make a big, bright finish to your show. A wand that Justine has been using right through her show miraculously grows into a tree, even taller than her, with a beautiful red flower on top. What a finale!

Try out making paper trees using old sheets of newspaper before trying it with good-quality paper. Do not roll the paper too tightly.

With care and a little twisting you can push the tree back into itself and so use it more than once.

If you plan to do the trick several times you could get your outer "wand paper" photocopied to save you painting it each time.

YOU WILL NEED THESE PROPS

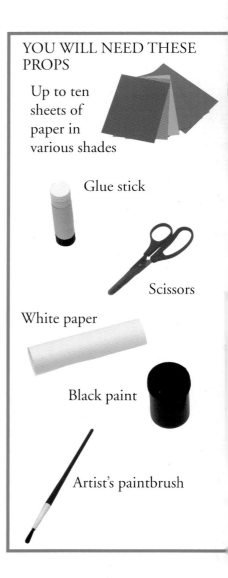

Up to ten sheets of paper in various shades

Glue stick

Scissors

White paper

Black paint

Artist's paintbrush